HOW SMART ARE YOU?

TEST YOUR
HISTORY
IQ

Erik Bruun

BLACK DOG & LEVENTHAL PUBLISHERS
NEW YORK

Published by

Black Dog & Leventhal Publishers Inc.
151 West 19th Street
New York, New York 10011

Distributed by

Workman Publishing Company
708 Broadway
New York, New York 10003

ISBN: 0-9637056-6-0

Contents

Introduction

Introduction

How smart are you? We can't answer that question for you generally, but this book certainly can determine your standing among the world's leading historians—or at least with some of your more competitive family members and friends.

After taking the quizzes spanning Dabbler, Smarter-Than-Most, and Genius levels, calculating exactly what kind of masterful grasp of history you have will be the easy part.

Each level has sixty-six or sixty-seven questions totaling two hundred questions in all. To get a true reading of your ability, take the tests adhering to the allotted time limits stated at the beginning of each section. Almost all of the questions are all multiple choice. There are no tricks, just compelling, fascinating, and strange historical trivia.

Once you complete a test, check the answer key at the end of that section and tally up your scores. Now you are equipped with all the information you need to spin the wheel and verify in seconds where your level of mastery lies.

All you have to do is turn to the front cover, and line up the number you answered correctly in the window on the scoring wheel. There are windows for each test level, so you can see how you fared with the Dabbler, Smarter-Than-Most, and Genius questions, as well as cumulatively.

Dabbler Questions

Time limit: 60 minutes

1 **Who said "The business of America is business?"**

    a. Calvin Coolidge
    b. Thomas Edison
    c. Henry Ford
    d. Herbert Hoover
    e. Theodore Roosevelt

2 **Which American Civil War battle gave Abraham Lincoln the confidence to declare the Emancipation Proclamation, freeing slaves in secessionist Confederate states?**

    a. Battle of Antietam
    b. Battle of Gettysburg
    c. Second Bull Run
    d. Battle of Shiloh
    e. Siege of Vicksburg

3 **Where was the "Valley of Death" of literary and military fame?**

    a. Little Big Horn
    b. Sevastapol
    c. Troy
    d. Valley Forge
    e. Verdun

4 **Who does not fit in this group of figures: Calvin Coolidge, Gerald Ford, Theodore Roosevelt, Harry S Truman, or John Tyler?**

5 **Match the song with the war and the nation:**

1. "Battle Hymn of the Republic"	a. Confederate States in American Civil War
2. "Boogie Woogie Bugle Boy"	b. Great Britain in World War I
3. "Dixie"	c. U.S. in World War I
4. "Over There"	d. U.S. in World War II
5. "Tipperary"	e. U.S. in Civil War

6 The first democratic republic was in. . .

   a. Athens
   b. China
   c. Florence
   d. Rome
   e. United States of America

7 Who commanded the first voyage around the world?

   a. John Cabot
   b. Christopher Columbus
   c. Sir Francis Drake
   d. Vasco da Gama
   e. Ferdinand Magellan

8 Who does not fit in this group?

   a. James Buchanan
   b. Jefferson Davis
   c. Ulysses S. Grant
   d. Andrew Johnson
   e. Abraham Lincoln

9 Between 1650 and 1850 the population of every major continent more than doubled with the exception of one. What continent declined in population?

   a. Africa
   b. Asia
   c. Europe
   d. North America
   e. South America

10 Which of the following monarchs was not a member of the Tudor family that reigned in Great Britain throughout the 16th century?

   a. Edward V
   b. Elizabeth I
   c. Henry VIII
   d. Mary I
   e. Mary Queen of Scots

11 **Which of these men signed the Declaration of Independence?**

a. Alexander Hamilton
b. Benjamin Franklin
c. Patrick Henry
d. Thomas Paine
e. George Washington

12 **What business sector provided the foundation for the city of Florence's economic success in the 15th and 16th centuries?**

a. The opening of Europe's first stock exchange
b. Mining
c. Textiles
d. Gelato production
e. Trade with the East

13 **Which of the following was not a reason that Texans fought for their independence from Mexico in 1836?**

a. Texas was populated by more settlers from the United States than from Mexico.
b. Many Texans sought independence as a step toward becoming annexed by the United States.
c. Mexico prohibited slavery.
d. Anger over the massacre of 187 men at the Alamo in a previous local revolt.
e. Mexican President Santa Ana proposed a new constitution to unify all of the Mexican territories.

14 **If you were a member of the Know Nothing Party in the 1850s in the U.S. you were. . .**

a. Against supporting education with public funds.
b. An avowed anti-Catholic who was alarmed at the immigration of so many Irish.
c. An advocate of isolationism and keeping the United States out of European affairs.
d. An abolitionist who sought the prohibition of slavery.
e. A women's rights supporter who lobbied for the right of women to vote.

15 Which of the following events does not fit?

a. Columbus discovers America for the Spanish throne.
b. The Spanish Armada is launched.
c. Spain expels the Muslims.
d. Jews are banished from Spain.
e. Spain is unified under the leadership of Isabel and Ferdinand.

16 Meiji Japan refers to which era in Japanese history?

a. The rapid modernization of Japan in the late 19th century.
b. The militaristic pre-World War II regime.
c. Post-World War II Japan.
d. Isolationist 17th and 18th century Japan.
e. Feudal Japan when the Samurai tradition was at its height.

17 The "10 days that shook the world" refer to. . .

a. Germany's Blitzkreig of France.
b. The outbreak of the Korean War.
c. The European revolutions of 1848.
d. The 1917 Russian Revolution.
e. The 1789 French Revolution.

18 Which French Revolutionary leader was most responsible for the Reign of Terror?

a. Napoleon Bonaparte
b. Jacques-Louis David
c. Marquis de Lafayette
d. Mirabeau
e. Maximilien Robespierre

19 Which of the signers of the Declaration of Independence lived the longest after July 4, 1776?

a. John Adams
b. John Hancock
c. Thomas Jefferson
d. Lewis Morris
e. Roger Sherman

20 **When and where was the Easter Rebellion?**

    a. South Africa, 1901
    b. China, 1906
    c. Ireland, 1916
    d. Russia, 1917
    e. Germany, 1920

21 **The Spanish Civil War was fought between. . .**

    a. Catholics and non-Catholics
    b. Loyalists to an existing republican government and
       monarchists, the military and the Church.
    c. Loyalists to an existing republican government and
       communists.
    d. Loyalists to the Catholic Church and the military.
    e. Loyalists to the existing Franco dictatorship and
       communists.

22 **What do Leon Trotsky, James Garfield, Caligula, Julius Caesar and Mohandas Gandhi have in common?**

23 **Which Jewish leader succeeded in unifying ancient Israel in the face of attacks from other tribes about 1000 B.C.?**

    a. David
    b. Jonathan
    c. Moses
    d. Saul
    e. Solomon

24 **Hannibal was a great general from . . . ?**

    a. Athens
    b. Carthage
    c. Macedonia
    d. Rome
    e. Sparta

25 Who was the first Roman emperor to become a Christian?

   a. Augustus
   b. Julius Caesar
   c. Constantine
   d. Nero
   e. Valentinian I

26 What great army did Genghis Khan organize and lead in its conquest of Asia and, later, part of Europe?

   a. The Aryans
   b. The Huns
   c. Manchu Empire
   d. The Mongols
   e. Seljuk Turks

27 What does the term "kamikaze" traditionally mean and refer to in Japanese history?

   a. It means "attack" and refers to the suicide charges by Samurai knights.
   b. It means "divine wind" and refers to a typhoon that decimated an invading fleet bearing Mongol hordes.
   c. It means "suicide" and refers to Japanese sailors who steered their ships into Portuguese ships in the 17th century.
   d. It means "divine wind" and refers to the storm that helped the Japanese defeat the Russians in the Battle of Port Arthur in 1904.
   e. It means "attack" and refers to Japanese pilots who used daring tactics to get as close to U.S. ships during World War II as possible before dropping their load of bombs.

28 Which Supreme Court case determined that the segregation of races on the basis of "separate but equal" was unconstitutional?

   a. *Brown vs. Board of Education of Topeka*
   b. The Dredd Scott decision
   c. *Marbury vs. Madison*
   d. *Plessy vs. Ferguson*
   e. *Worcester vs. Georgia*

29 Who coined the term "iron curtain" in reference to the influence of the Soviet Union over Eastern Europe?

    a. Winston Churchill
    b. Anthony Eden
    c. Joseph McCarthy
    d. Franklin D. Roosevelt
    e. Harry S Truman

30 Who does not fit in this group?

    a. Omar Bradley
    b. Dwight "Ike" Eisenhower
    c. Douglas MacArthur
    d. George Patton
    e. "Black Jack" Pershing

31 Where was the capital of the Byzantine Empire?

    a. Athens
    b. Baghdad
    c. Constantinople
    d. Rhodes
    e. Ankara

32 What feat opened the floodgates of trade to the Great Lakes in the early 19th century?

    a. The invention of the steamboat by Robert Fulton
    b. The Treaty of Ghent ending the War of 1812 eliminated tariffs between Canada and the United States that had previously obstructed trade.
    c. The completion of the Erie Canal in 1825
    d. The defeat of the Creeks at Horseshoe Bend in 1814
    e. The construction of rail lines linking New York City with Montreal

33 Who does not fit in this group of figures who made the headlines during the McCarthy era in the late 1940s and early 1950s in the U.S.?

    a. Roy Cohn
    b. Dashiell Hammett
    c. Owen Lattimore
    d. George C. Marshall
    e. John Service

34 Why was the Triangle Shirtwaist Company significant to United States history?

a. It was the first company to employ modern factory techniques developed in England for a textile company in Lowell, Massachusetts, thus ushering in the Industrial Revolution in New England.
b. Its production of uniforms for Union soldiers in the Civil War was riddled with fraudulent practices that led to a crackdown on war profiteers and public accountability.
c. A fire at the company's New York City factory in 1911 killed 146 women who could not escape the building because of improper safety precautions, leading to an era of workplace reforms.
d. A Communist-inspired riot at the company's New York City factory in the early 1920s led to the death of dozens of striking workers.
e. The company employed a spirited woman who helped organize one of the first effective unions in a southern textile mill. The story inspired the making of the movie "Norma Rae."

35 What European city became the home of the Pope in 1305 and eventually competed with Rome for the permanent center of the Catholic Church for many years?

a. Avignon
b. Madrid
c. Milan
d. Naples
e. Paris

36 Which devastating event had a great impact on 14th century Europe?

a. The Thirty Years' War
b. An invasion of the Mongol hordes from the Far East
c. The Bubonic Plague
d. An invasion of Islamic armies through Greece
e. The Spanish Inquisition

37 **Who were the major adversaries in the War of Roses?**

    a. The Cavaliers and the Roundheads
    b. The House of Tudor and the House of Stuart
    c. England and France
    d. England and Scotland
    e. The House of York and the House of Lancaster

38 **How did Joan of Arc come to the rescue of France?**

    a. She lifted the siege of Orléans by the English in 1429.
    b. She led French troops at the Battle of Crecy in 1346.
    c. She united the Protestant Huguenots with the ruling Catholics in the early 1500s.
    d. She put down rioters in Paris that threatened the Dauphin in 1358.
    e. She led the French troops against Henry V at the Battle of Agincourt in 1415.

39 **Who were the first non-aboriginals to settle Alaska?**

    a. British explorers
    b. Canadian fur trappers
    c. New England whalers
    d. Russian fur trappers
    e. United States gold prospectors

40 **Who was Lao-tse?**

    a. The founder of Buddhism
    b. The founder of Taoism
    c. The first Chinese emperor of the M'ing Dynasty
    d. The leader of the Long March in the Chinese Communist Revolution
    e. The founder of Hinduism

41 **Who was the Sun King?**

    a. Charlemagne
    b. Henry VIII
    c. Louis XIV
    d. Napoleon III
    e. King Tutankamen

42 Which of the following events did not occur in the 14th century?

  a. Dante Alighieri wrote *The Divine Comedy*.
  b. Paper, which is first invented in China in the 2nd century A.D., is produced in Europe and soon replaces vellum as the medium for manuscripts and books.
  c. Joan of Arc, a shepherd from Lorraine, led a French army and drives the English out of Orléans.
  d. The Hundred Years' War begins.
  e. The Black Death ravages Europe killing one third of the population of Europe.

43 Which of the following was not true about Dracula?

  a. He lived in a castle in Transylvania.
  b. A Christian, he is credited with killing 24,000 Muslims in the Balkans.
  c. He slept in a box in the dark during daylight.
  d. He was known as Vlad the Impaler.
  e. His response to a pair of visiting ambassadors who refused to take their hats off to him, as it was not their custom, was to nail the hats to the ambassadors' heads.

44 Who were the first and last czars of Russia?

  a. Peter the Great and Nicholas II
  b. Peter the Great and Alexander II
  c. Peter the Great and Rasputin
  d. Ivan the Terrible and Nicholas II
  e. Ivan the Terrible and Alexander II

45 Which Roman converted to Judaism and was married 10 times?

  a. Pontius Pilate
  b. Caligula
  c. Constantine
  d. Herod
  e. Hadrian

46 Who was El Cid?

a. A Spanish king in the 10th century who unified Christian Spaniards against the Muslims.

b. A renegade Spanish knight who battled, and often slaughtered, Muslims during the 11th century.

c. A Spanish king who joined the Muslims in the 10th century to help them expand northward to the Pyrenees mountains.

d. A Basque prince who fought the unification of Spain by Isabel and Ferdinand in the late 15th century.

e. A mythical figure in Spanish literature.

47 Match the 15th and 16th century explorer with his respective accomplishment.

1. Vasco de Balboa
2. John Cabot
3. Hernan Cortes
4. Vasco da Gama
5. Prince Henry the Navigator
6. Francisco Pizarro

a. He discovered the Pacific Ocean.

b. A noted Portuguese who developed the exploration of West Africa

c. He led a Spanish expedition to defeat the Inca Empire.

d. He led the first European expedition to North America since the Vikings.

e. He led a Spanish expedition to defeat the Aztec empire.

f. He was the first European to sail around the Cape of Good Hope to reach India.

48 Who invented the movable type printing press?

a. Firmin Didot

b. Erasmus of Rotterdam

c. Johannes Gutenberg

d. William Caxton

e. R. R. Donnelley

49 All of the following presidents were childless with the exception of which one?

a. Calvin Coolidge
b. Warren Harding
c. Andrew Jackson
d. George Washington
e. Woodrow Wilson

50 In Spanish history, which of the following nations or groups did not conquer the Iberian Peninsula?

a. France
b. Hapsburg Empire
c. Islamic Empire
d. Roman Empire
e. The Visgoths

51 What sparked the Indian Mutiny of 1857-58?

a. The conscription of Indians into the British Army
b. Feuds between Hindu and Muslim tribes within the British Army
c. Refusal by Indians to participate in the opium trade
d. Resentment by Indians that the British refused to participate in the opium trade
e. Widespread refusal by Indian troops to bite open ammunition cartridges greased with pork and beef fats forbidden to Muslims and Hindus

52 Who brought an end to the hyperinflation that plagued the German economy in the early 1920s?

a. Adolph Hitler
b. Franz von Papen
c. Paul von Hindenburg
d. Wilhelm I
e. A coalition of international bankers put together as part of the Treaty of Versailles to direct the German economy.

53 What European nation occupied by Germany during World War II solidly refused to collaborate with Nazi efforts to exterminate Jews?

    a. Czechoslovakia
    b. Denmark
    c. France
    d. Norway
    e. The Netherlands

54 Match the following acquisitions of territory by the United States with the with the dates:

    1. California   a. 1803
    2. Florida   b. 1818
    3. Gadsden Purchase   c. 1845
    4. Louisiana Purchase d. 1848
    5. Texas   e. 1853

55 Who was the first human being to go into space?

    a. Neil Armstrong
    b. Yuri Gagarin
    c. John Glenn
    d. Alan B. Shepard, Jr.
    e. Georgi Kosmonot

56 Which lawyer presented the case for integration in the Supreme Court in *Brown vs. Board of Education of Topeka*?

    a. Roy Wilkins
    b. Clarence Darrow
    c. Medgar Evers
    d. Thurgood Marshall
    e. Drew Days II

57 Which of the following is not one of the ancient Seven Wonders of the World?

    a. The Colossus of Rhodes
    b. The Great Wall of China
    c. The Hanging Gardens of Babylon
    d. The Pyramids of Egypt
    e. The Statue of Zeus at Olympia

58 Red, white and blue are among the most common colors on national flags. Which of the following countries does not have red, white and blue on its flag?

   a. Czechoslovakia
   b. France
   c. Germany
   d. Russia
   e. United Kingdom

59 Where were Czar Nicholas II and his family murdered by the Bolsheviks?

   a. Ekaterinaburg
   b. Kiev
   c. Kursk
   d. Odessa
   e. Tobolsk

60 Which of the following did not lose his or her head during the French Revolution?

   a. Marie Antoinette
   b. George Jacques Danton
   c. Marquis de Lafayette
   d. Louis XVI
   e. Maximilien Robespierre

61 Which of the following was not known primarily as a critic of his times?

   a. Honoré de Balzac
   b. Honoré Daumier
   c. Charles Dickens
   d. Francisco José de Goya
   e. William Wordsworth

62 Since biblical times Jerusalem has been ruled by many nations. Which of the following never governed Jerusalem?

   a. The Crusaders
   b. England
   c. France
   d. Jordan
   e. The Ottoman Empire

63 Who was the first person to sail through the Arctic Northwest Passage?

    a. Roald Amundsen
    b. Salomon A. Andree
    c. Sir Francis Bacon
    d. Capt. James Cook
    e. Robert E. Peary

64 Who was the first person to land on Antarctica?

    a. Roald Amundsen
    b. Richard E. Byrd
    c. Capt. James Cook
    d. Leonard Kristensen
    e. Robert F. Scott

65 With which of the following Third World countries did the Soviet Union not succeed in establishing a military base or close military ties during the Cold War?

    a. Algeria
    b. Cuba
    c. Egypt
    d. Guinea
    e. Lebanon

66 Match the following Union generals in the American Civil War with the battles they commanded:

1. George G. Meade	a. Antietam
2. Ambrose E. Burnside	b. Second Manassas
3. U lysses S. Grant	c. Gettysburg
4. George B. MacClellan	d. Fredericksburg
5. John Pope	e. Vicksburg

Dabbler Answer Sheet

(Score 1 point for each correct answer unless otherwise indicated.)

1. a
2. a
3. b. The battle of Sevastapol was immortalized in Tennyson's poem "The Charge of the Light Brigade."
4.   Gerald Ford. Ford succeeded Richard Nixon who resigned from office. The others became president upon the death of their predecessors.
5. 1e, 2d, 3a, 4c, 5b
6. a
7. e
8. b. Jefferson Davis was the first and only president of the Confederate States of America. All the others served as presidents of the United States.
9. a
10. e. Mary, Queen of Scots was a Stuart, a cousin of Elizabeth I. She was the mother of James I who became king of England after Elizabeth I died in 1603.
11. b
12. c
13. d. The Alamo was the site of a battle *during* the War for Texan Independence.
14. b
15. b. The Spanish Armada was fought in 1588. The rest of the events took place in the 15th century.
16. a
17. d
18. e
19. a. John Adams died hours after Thomas Jefferson on the 50th anniversary of the signing of the Declaration of Independence, which they co-authored, on July 4, 1826. His last words were poignantly but inaccurately "Thomas Jefferson still survives."
20. c
21. b
22.   They were all assassinated.
23. a
24. b
25. c
26. d
27. b
28. d
29. a

30. e.   "Black Jack" Pershing commanded the U.S. Army in Europe during World War I. The others were World War II generals.

31. b

32. c

33. c

34. a.   Roy Cohn worked on Senator McCarthy's staff. The others were brought under criticism and scrutiny by McCarthy and his followers.

35. a

36. c

37. e

38. a

39. d

40. b

41. c

42. c.   Joan of Arc takes Orléans in 1429.

43. c.   Bela Lugosi, an actor who played Dracula, did.

44. a

45. d

46. c

47. 1a,   2d,   3e,   4f,   5b,   6c

48. c

49. a

50. b.   The Hapsburgs ruled Spain through alliances and marriages culminating with the reign of Charles V.

51. e

52. b

53. b

54. 1d,   2b,   3e,   4a,   5c

55. b

56. d

57. b

58. c

59. a

60. c

61. e

62. c

63. a

64. d

65. e

66. 1c,   2d,   3e,   4a,   5b

Smarter-Than-Most Questions

Time limit: 60 minutes

1 **What do these American presidents have in common: Bill Clinton, Rutherford B. Hayes, Abraham Lincoln, Richard Nixon and Woodrow Wilson?**

2 **Who sanctioned the murder of Thomás Becket in 1170 while he was delivering vespers in the Salisbury Cathedral?**

a. Henry I
b. Henry II
c. Henry III
d. Henry IV
e. Henry V

3 **Place in chronological order the six wives of Henry VIII:**

a. Anne Boleyn
b. Anne of Cleves
c. Catherine of Aragon
d. Catherine Howard
e. Catherine Parr
f. Jane Seymour

4 **Match each wife of Henry VIII with her fate:**

1. Anne Boleyn
2. Anne of Cleves
3. Catherine of Aragon
4. Catherine Howard

5. Catherine Parr
6. Jane Seymour

a. Died of natural causes
b. Beheaded first
c. Beheaded second
d. Divorced immediately after Henry VIII established the Church of England
e. Divorced
f. Outlived Henry VIII

5 Where was the first civilization to have an ordered society that included cities and an organized government?

   a. East Africa
   b. Indus Valley
   c. Mesopotamia
   d. Nile Valley
   e. Peking

6 Which of the following languages are not spoken by at least I million people in Latin or South America?

   a. Guarani
   b. Catalan
   c. Portuguese
   d. Quecha
   e. Spanish

7 Which of the following lands did Columbus not visit?

   a. The Bahamas
   b. Cuba
   c. Hispanola
   d. The Barbados
   e. Puerto Rico

8 Which best describes the positions held by Edmund Burke?

   a. He was sympathetic to the causes of the American Revolution and the French Revolution.
   b. He was sympathetic to the cause of the American Revolution but he opposed the French Revolution.
   c. He was opposed to the American Revolution but he was sympathetic to the French Revolution.
   d. He opposed both the American Revolution and the French Revolution.
   e. He changed his views on both the American Revolution and the French Revolution. In both cases he was an early supporter but as the struggles progressed he became increasingly opposed to the causes.

9 **Which of the following rebellions does not belong in this group?**

a. American Revolution
b. The Boxer Rebellion
c. The Great Indian Mutiny
d. Mau-Mau
e. Shays's Rebellion

10 **Which African nation played a significant role in Ancient Greek and Roman civilizations but was later isolated from its ties to the Hellenistic communities by the Islamic tide that swept the Middle East?**

a. Cameroon
b. Ethiopia
c. Kenya
d. Morocco
e. Nigeria

11 **Which one of the following accomplishments was not achieved by the Lincoln Administration during the American Civil War?**

a. Making land readily available to western farmers through the Homestead Act
b. The freeing of slaves in the United States
c. Initiating the construction of a transcontinental railroad
d. Raising tariffs
e. The implementation of the first national draft

12 **How long was the Thirty Years' War?**

a. 28 years
b. 29 years
c. 30 years
d. 31 years
e. 32 years

13 How long was the Hundred Years' War?

    a. 96 years
    b. 100 years
    c. 106 years
    d. 116 years
    e. 122 years

14 Which of the following best describes Napoleon Bonaparte's height?

    a. He was of exceedingly short stature.
    b. He was slightly shorter than the average European man in the late 18th century.
    c. His height was almost precisely average for his time.
    d. He was slightly taller than most other European men.
    e. He was very tall compared to the average height of European males at the time.

15 Which of the following descriptions about Napoleon Bonaparte's invasion of Russia in 1812 is inaccurate?

    a. Hundreds, if not thousands, of soldiers died during the summer of heat exhaustion and sunstroke.
    b. Napoleon's army suffered from a poor supply system and bad tactical planning.
    c. Napoleon's army fled Moscow almost two weeks before the first frost.
    d. An unusually harsh winter froze thousands of French soldiers to death, decimating the army.
    e. The Russians successfully swept down on Napoleon as his army attempted to cross the Beresina River.

16 Airplanes first appeared as weapons in which of the following conflicts?

    a. The Italo-Turkish War
    b. The First Balkan War
    c. The Mexican Revolution
    d. The Russo-Japanese War
    e. World War I

17 Which of the following scientists did not work on the Manhattan Project in building the atomic bomb at Los Alamos, New Mexico?

a. J. Robert Oppenheimer
b. Enrico Fermi
c. Leo Szilard
d. Edward Teller
e. General Leslie R. Groves

18 Where was the first university established in North America?

a. Boston
b. Philadelphia
c. Mexico City
d. Williamsburg
e. Santo Domingo

19 Where did the United States fight its first major battle using helicopters to transport soldiers in and out of a combat zone?

a. Dien Bien Phu
b. Hue
c. Ia Drang
d. Pork Chop Hill
e. Saigon

20 Who was Archduke Ferdinand Maximilian Joseph?

a. An archduke assassinated in Sarajevo, triggering a chain of events that led to World War I
b. A successful Austrian commander during the Napoleonic Wars
c. An Austrian adventurer who ruled Mexico on behalf of France in the 1860s but was eventually killed by a Mexican firing squad
d. A German prince who claims to be the current king of Romania
e. Emperor Joseph II prior to becoming the ruling monarch of Austro-Hungary

21 Which of the following areas was not a combat zone during World War I?

a. East Africa
b. Germany
c. Palestine
d. Persia
e. Russia

22 What percentage of the 5,462 American deaths in the Spanish-American War were the result of battle casualties?

a. 6 percent
b. 25 percent
c. 50 percent
d. 70 percent
e. 95 percent

23 What was the last foreign army to invade the United States?

a. Canada
b. England
c. France
d. Mexico
e. Spain

24 Match the following European monarchs and presidents with the nation they ruled at the outbreak of World War II.

1. Christian X
2. Gustavus V
3. Haakon VII
4. Leopold III
5. Ignacy Moscicki
6. Wilhelmina

a. Belgium
b. Denmark
c. Holland
d. Norway
e. Poland
f. Sweden

25 Which of the following descriptions cannot be applied to Richard The Lion-Hearted, King of England?

    a. He slaughtered 3,000 Muslim captives including women and children.
    b. He seized Jerusalem as head of the crusaders.
    c. He bankrupted England.
    d. He was imprisoned by Leopold of Austria as a prisoner of war.
    e. He spent less than two years in England as king and never learned how to speak English.

26 Where did the James-Younger gang meet its end?

    a. Dodge City
    b. Northfield
    c. The OK Corral
    d. Tombstone
    e. Tucson

27 Who said the following? "The problem of the 20th century is the problem of the color line."

    a. W. E. B. DuBois
    b. Marcus Garvey
    c. Martin Luther King, Jr.
    d. Malcolm X
    e. Booker T. Washington

28 Who of the following died differently from the others?

    a. Marc Antony
    b. Julius Caesar
    b. Cicero
    d. Licinus Crassus
    e. Pompey

29 When Charlemagne united Europe in the late 8th century and early 9th century he established the capital of the Holy Roman Empire at. . .

   a. Aix-la-Chapelle
   b. Cologne
   c. Paris
   d. Reims
   e. Rome

30 Where did the Huns originate?

   a. Hungary
   b. Mongolia
   c. Siberia
   d. Tibet
   e. Uzbekistan

31 During which 100-year period did the Islamic Empire conquer all of northern Africa, the entire Middle East, Spain, southern France and western India?

   a. 500-600
   b. 630-730
   c. 660-760
   d. 690-790
   e. 830-930

32 Who was Publius?

   a. A great Roman orator
   b. The last Roman emperor
   c. The collective pen name of Alexander Hamilton, James Madison and John Jay who wrote a series of essays known as the Federalist Papers advocating the ratification of the U.S. Constitution
   d. The collective pen name of Alexander Hamilton, James Madison and John Jay who wrote a series of essays known as the Federalist Papers arguing against the ratification of the U.S. Constitution
   e. The collective pen name of Patrick Henry, Aaron Burr and John Hancock who wrote a series of essays known as the Federalist Papers advocating ratification of the U.S. Constitution

33 Who was the only United States president to serve in the House of Representatives after his presidential term was completed?

34 Match the following American gangsters with the circumstances surrounding their deaths:

1. Legs Diamond	a. Shot by five steel-plated bullets while asleep in bed
2. John Dillinger	b. Shot down in a hail of gunfire by FBI agents in front of a movie theater where he was going to see a movie with the girlfriend who had betrayed him to police
3. Pretty Boy Floyd	c. Shot in Barrington, Illinois, by two FBI agents who were themselves killed by this gangster's Thompson machine gun in the exchange of fire
4. Baby Face Nelson	d. Shot by fellow gangsters of Murder Inc. who wanted to prevent him from carrying out a pledge to murder New York special prosecutor Thomas Dewey
5. Dutch Schultz	e. Died of heart failure surrounded by his family

35 How old was Mary, Queen of Scots when she became Queen of Scotland?

   a. 1 week
   b. 6 months
   c. 6 years
   d. 12 years
   e. 16 years

36 How many days were American citizens held hostage in the U. S. Embassy in Teheran by the Iranian revolutionaries that overthrew the Shah?

a. 222 days
b. 333 days
c. 388 days
d. 444 days
e. 488 days

37 Who expanded the Persian Empire to its height in the 6th century BC?

a. Artaxerxes
b. Cyrus the Great
c. Darius I
d. Darius II
e. Teispes

38 Who were the adversaries at the Battle of Marathon?

a. Alexander the Great's Macedonian Army versus the Persian Empire
b. Rome versus the Carthaginians
c. Athens versus the Persian Empire
d. Marc Anthony versus Octavius
e. Sparta versus Athens

39 What was the last Imperial Dynasty to rule China?

a. Ch'in
b. Ch'ing
c. Ming
d. T'ang
e. Yuan

40 **When and why did the Japanese ban international trade and travel?**

    a. 1235 for fear of the influence of Buddhism on the Japanese Shinto culture

    b. 1312 as a tactic to prevent the Mongol Empire from invading

    c. 1567 as a tactic to prevent the Manchu Empire from dominating Japanese internal trade

    d. 1635 to prevent the influence of Christianity from undermining Japanese culture

    e. Japan has never banned international trade and travel.

41 **What was the cause of the First Opium War?**

    a. China's attempt to clamp down on the illegal opium trade carried on by the British for Chinese customers

    b. Britain's attempt to clamp down on the illegal opium trade carried on by the Chinese for Chinese customers

    c. India's attempt to open new markets in China for the sale of opium

    d. United States intervention in Colombia to clamp down on the drug trade

    e. A British decision to destroy more than 100,000 pounds of opium in Canton by burning it

42 **If you were a member of the Imperial Diet you were. . .**

    a. An elected representative in the first German Parliament

    b. An elected representative in the first Japanese Parliament

    c. Part of the Ch'ing Dynasty's court of intrigue in the 19th century

    d. Part of the King of Siam's court

    e. One of the "Four Hundred" who ruled Athens

43 What was the "Hundred Flowers" campaign?

a. An agrarian reform movement spearheaded by Mao Tse-tung

b. An organized purge of Communist China's leadership in the 1960s

c. A campaign to rid China of most of its birds to boost grain crops

d. The final military campaign by the Communists that ousted Chiang Kai-shek's Nationalist Army from mainland China

e. A short stint of time in the 1950s when Mao Tse-tung encouraged self-criticism of the Chinese government

44 Match the following labor/socialist leaders with the union or cause they advocated:

1. Eugene Debs
2. Samuel Gompers
3. "Big Bill" Haywood
4. Jimmy Hoffa
5. John Lewis

a. American Federation of Labor
b. Committee of Industrial Organizations
c. Industrial Workers of the World
d. Socialist Party
e. Teamsters

45 Match these American generals with the battles they fought:

1. Benedict Arnold
2. Horatio Gates
3. Nathaniel Greene
4. William Prescott
5. George Washington

a. Bunker Hill
b. Cowpens
c. Princeton
d. The Seige of Quebec
e. Saratoga

46 Match each of the following "robber barons" with the industry in which he first made his fortune during the late 19th century in the United States:

1. Andrew Carnegie
2. Henry Frick
3. J. P. Morgan
4. John D. Rockefeller
5. Cornelius Vanderbilt

a. Banking
b. Coke
c. Oil
d. Railroads
e. Steel

47 What was the Missouri Compromise?

a. A legislative deal in the United States Congress by which slavery status in new states would be determined by "popular sovereignity" in the territory

b. The decision to allow Kansas and Nebraska to determine whether they would be slave or non-slave states through popular ballot

c. The agreement which affirmed Missouri's loyalty to the Union while keeping its status as a slave state

d. A treaty allowing Native Americans to remain in the Missouri territories while United States settlers would be permitted to go to other areas west of the Mississippi without fear of attack

e. An agreement in the United States Senate which allowed Missouri into the Union as a slave state and Maine as a non-slave state to maintain the balance of slave and non-slave state votes

48 Which was the first state to be admitted to the United States? Which was the last?

49 When and why was the National Association for the Advancement of Colored People founded?

a. 1868 in Boston by black leaders including Frederick Douglass and former abolitionists who started an organization to assist former slaves make the adjustment to life as free people

b. 1875 in Tuscaloosa, Alabama, by a group of elected black officials who were concerned with the rise of the Ku Klux Klan and the pending end of the Reconstruction Era

c. 1877 in Boston by a group of black and white leaders alarmed at the conclusion of the Reconstruction Era, the rise of the Ku Klux Klan and the emergence of Jim Crow laws

d. 1909 in New York City by a group of white and black intellectuals who wanted to take an aggressive approach to advancing racial equality as opposed to Booker T. Washington's theory of gradualism in race relations

e. 1923 in New York City by a group of black nationalists who advocated the mass migration of blacks to Africa

50 Mark I was the first electronic computer. It was 50 feet long and 8 feet high, weighed 30 tons and used 18,000 vacuum tubes. What was it used for?

a. German engineers designed the computer during World War II to determine the speed and trajectory of V-1 and V-2 rockets.

b. Japanese engineers designed the computer after World War II as part of a public-private venture to give Japanese industry an early jump in the technological revolution.

c. It was developed by Princeton University and the U.S. Department of Commerce to sort and analyze the 1940 census.

d. IBM and Harvard engineers designed the computer during World War II to determine the speed and trajectory of artillery shells aimed at enemy airplanes and other targets.

e. American engineers working with the Manhattan Project developed the computer to calculate the decomposition of the uranium and plutonium nuclei in the design of the first atomic bomb.

51 What Danish king ruled a kingdom from his seat in Winchester, England, that stretched from Iceland to Scandinavia to the Baltic states in the early 1000s?

a. Eric the Red
b. Leif Ericson
c. Knut
d. Harold I
e. William the Conqueror

52 Which United States president was elected despite a smear campaign against him that included the chant "Ma, ma, where's my pa?" in reference to an illegitimate child he fathered?

a. Grover Cleveland
b. Warren Harding
c. Benjamin Harrison
d. Rutherford B. Hayes
e. John F. Kennedy

53 Which of the following products did Europeans not import from the New World as part of the Columbian Exchange?

a. Cocoa
b. Corn
c. Horses
d. Potatoes
e. Tobacco

54 True or false: Jews dominated the money lending business in Europe during the Middle Ages.

55 Which of the following inventions does not belong?

a. The compass
b. Gun powder
c. Mechanical clocks
d. Paper
e. Taxi meters

56 Who were the dominant European military superpowers of the 15th and 16th centuries?

a. England and France
b. Germany and France
c. England and the Ottoman Empire
d. The Hapsburg Empire and the Ottoman Empire
e. The Hapsburg Empire and England

57 An 18th century writer was thrown into jail in the American colonies for his writings in the local press. His trial and resulting acquittal for alleged seditious libel established the American tradition of freedom of the press. Who was the writer?

a. John Player Crosby
b. Benjamin Franklin
c. Thomas Paine
d. John Edward Sparks
e. John Peter Zenger

58 **What happened in the Massacre of St. Bartholomew's Day in 1572?**

    a. Bohemian Protestants threw two imperial regents from the window of the Prague council room, in protest against the lifting of religious toleration in Bohemia.

    b. Spurred on by "Bloody Queen" Mary I, British Catholics rounded up dozens of Protestants and burned them at the stake.

    c. By order of Catherine de Medici, French Catholics killed scores of French Protestants (Huguenots), thus sparking a civil war.

    d. Followers of Martin Luther massacred residents of a German Catholic village that refused to denounce the Pope, thus starting religious wars that divided Europe for decades.

    e. By order of Philip II of Spain, hundreds of Muslims were massacred as pagans.

59 **Which of the following was not a reason for the Dutch "economic miracle" that allowed the tiny Netherlands to become a dominant naval world power of the 1600s?**

    a. The establishment of the Bank of Netherlands in 1609 as the first national bank to offer international exchange and credit facilities

    b. Modern military technology that gave Dutch armies and navies a military prowess disproportional to the number of soldiers and ships available to the nation

    c. A policy of religious toleration that attracted such prosperous fugitives from religious persecution as Jews and French Huguenots

    d. Technical expertise in shipbuilding and insurance

    e. The decline of Portugal and Spain as sea powers

60 **Who does not fit in this group of political leaders?**

    a. Charles I

    b. Ferdinand Maximillian Joseph

    c. James II

    d. Louis XVI

    e. Nicholas II

61 Which of the following did not contribute to the start of the Industrial Revolution in England in the 18th century?

a. A run of good harvests in the first half of the 18th century
b. A steady population increase due to increased birth rates and decreased death rates, thus increasing demand for consumption
c. An unusual stretch of peacetime allowing England to develop its colonies and invest in its domestic economy
d. Profits from foreign trade providing capital for domestic investment
e. The discovery of coke smelting in the 1730s by Abraham Darby enabling the mass production of cheap iron

62 1848 was a year of tremendous upheaval in Europe. A declining economy, poor harvest and urbanization had created an environment of discontent in which such new ideas as socialism, nationalism and democracy started to take hold. A series of revolutions took place throughout Europe. Which of the following cities did not become a center for revolution?

a. Budapest
b. Frankfurt
c. Prague
d. Rome
e. Warsaw

63 Which of the following people did not contribute to the unification of Italy in the mid-19th century?

a. Camillo di Cavour
b. Victor Emmanuel
c. Giuseppe Garibaldi
d. Giuseppe Mazzini
e. Pope Pius IX

64 Toulouse-Lautrec designed a poster at the turn of the 20th century for the first luxury consumer product sold to the mass market. What was the product?

a. Automobiles
b. Bicycles
c. Phonographs
d. Sewing machines
e. Typewriters

65 Which of the following musicians did not participate in the "Jazz Age" of the 1920s in the United States?

a. Louis Armstrong
b. Bix Biederbecke
c. George Gershwin
d. Charlie Parker
e. Paul Whiteman

66 Which of the following quotations is not attributed to Benjamin Franklin?

a. "Early to bed, early to rise, makes a man healthy, wealthy and wise."
b. "God helps them that help themselves."
c. "We must all hang together or assuredly we shall all hang separately."
d. "I begin to smell a rat."
e. "There was never a good war or a bad peace."

67 Who was the last United States president to not attend college?

a. Dwight D. Eisenhower
b. Lyndon B. Johnson
c. Abraham Lincoln
d. Ronald Reagan
e. Harry S Truman

Smarter-Than-Most Answers

(Score 1 point for each correct answer unless otherwise indicated.)

1.   None of these United States presidents was elected with a majority of the vote in his first successful election.

2. b

3. c, a, b, f, d, e
      Catherine of Aragon, Anne Boleyn, Jane Seymour, Anne of Cleves, Catherine Howard, Catherine Parr.

4. 1b,   2d,   3e,   4c,   5f,   6a

5. c

6. b

7. d

8. b

9. e   The other rebellions pitted oppressed colonies against colonial powers. Shays's Rebellion consisted of a group of farmers and former Revolutionary War veterans against the Massachusetts government in 1786.

10. b

11. b   The Emancipation Proclamation of 1862 freed slaves in secessionist Southern states. Slavery was not banned in the entire United States until the 13th Amendment was ratified Dec. 6, 1865, after the Civil War was over and President Lincoln had been assassinated.

12. c

13. d

14. c   He stood 5 feet 6 inches, the average height of men in the late 18th century.

15. d   The winter of 1812 was a mild one for Russia. Historians attribute the collapse of his army to a poor supply system and bad tactical planning. Napoleon and others blamed the weather to deflect responsibility from themselves.

16. a

17. c   Leo Szilard worked on the Manhattan Project at the Univeristy of Chicago, not at Los Alamos.

18. a   The first university in North America was founded in Mexico City in 1551.

19. c

20. c

21. b

22. a

23. d   Pancho Villa invaded New Mexico in 1916 with a renegade army he commanded. He killed a dozen American passengers aboard a train and murdered a group of American engineers.

24. 1b, 2f, 3d, 4a, 5e, 6c (1/2 point each)

25. b

26. b

27. b

28. a   Marc Anthony committed suicide. The rest were murdered.

29. a

30. b

31. b

32. c

33.   John Quincy Adams

34. 1e, 2a, 3b, 4c, 5d (1/2 point each)

35. a

36. d

37. b

38. c

39. b

40. d

41. a

42. b

43. e

44. 1d, 2a, 3c, 4e, 5b (1/2 point each)

45. 1d, 2e, 3b, 4a, 5c (1/2 point each)

46. 1e, 2b, 3a, 4c, 5d (1/2 point each)

47. e

48.   Delaware, Dec. 7, 1787; Hawaii, Aug. 21, 1959. (1/2 point each)

49. d

50. d

51. c

52. a

53. c   The Europeans brought horses to the New World where the animals swept across the North and South American continents more rapidly than European settlers.

54.   True. The Christian Church viewed money lending, or usury, as a sin. It was not until the Medici family in Florence became involved in banking that a significant amount of lending in Medieval Europe was done by non-Jews.

55. e   Romans invented the taxi meter, the Chinese invented the rest. The Roman taxi meter operated by using a series of gears rotated by the carriage's wheels. As the wheels rotated pebbles would drop into a holder. At the conclusion of the ride, the driver would count the number of pebbles to determine the cost of the ride.

56. d

57. e   John Peter Zenger wrote unrelenting attacks in his newspaper, the *New York Weekly Journal,* against New York Governor William Cosby accusing him of undermining the local court system and repeatedly breaking the laws of the colony and England.

58. c

59. b   The Dutch republic's economic success was based almost entirely on its economic, trading and technical expertise in commerce. The nation was often at war in the 1600s but, as often as not, lost. The downfall of the Dutch republic came about as its main rivals, England and France, succeeded in defeating the nation on the fields of battle.

60. c   James II. All the others were deposed through execution. The Catholic James II was deposed from the British throne in 1688 by his Protestant rivals, William and Mary, in the bloodless Glorious Revolution.

61. c   England was engaged in numerous wars throughout the century and lost its largest colonies because of the American Revolution at the end of the century.

62. e

63. e   The Vatican strongly resisted the unification of Italy as a divided Italy historically enhanced the power of the Pope. Although all of Italy except Rome was unified by 1866, it was not until France removed its troops from Rome in 1870, to fight in the Franco-Prussian War, that the Catholic Church allowed Rome and its surrounding terrain to become part of the unified Italy.

64. b

65. d   Charlie Parker was born in 1920 and was thus too young to participate in the Jazz Age of the 1920s.

66. d   This quote is from *Don Quixote* by Cervantes.

67. e

Genius Questions

Time limit: 60 minutes

1 **U.S. Secretary of State William Seward negotiated the purchase of the Virgin Islands from Denmark and the Alaska territories from Russia in 1867. Which property cost more and what was the price differential?**

2 **Gen. Douglas MacArthur was well known for his flamboyance and skills as a military leader. Which of the following traits or accomplishments cannot be attributed to him?**

    a. He went on a daring raid into Mexico in disguise to scout out Pancho Villa.

    b. He was popular with the Japanese as the Supreme Commander of Japan after having defeated them in World War II.

    c. He carried a pearl-handled pistol as a sidearm during the Korean War.

    d. He ran for the Presidency in 1952.

    e. He led a raid on "The Bonus Army" in Washington D.C. that resulted in the deaths of several World War I veterans and their family members including children.

3 **The Mexican War ended in 1848 with the signing of the Treaty of Guadalupe Hidalgo. What territories did the U. S. gain from this treaty?**

    a. All of modern California, Nevada, most of New Mexico and Arizona, and a large portion of Colorado

    b. All of modern California, Nevada, Utah, New Mexico and Arizona and a large portion of Colorado

    c. All of modern California, Nevada, Utah, New Mexico and Arizona

    d. All of modern California, Nevada and Utah, most of New Mexico and Arizona, and a large portion of Colorado

    e. All of modern California, Nevada, Utah, New Mexico and large portions of Arizona, Colorado and western Texas

4 What was the name of Alexander the Great's horse?

    a. Bucephalus
    b. Darius
    c. Pegasus
    d. Philippus
    e. Pytheas

5 Why is the Kolyma Basin historically noteworthy?

    a. It was the site where an enormous meteorite crashed in the last century devastating hundreds of square miles of Siberian forest.
    b. It was where the Russians secretly built thousands of T-34 tanks in World War II in preparation for counter-attacking the invading Germans.
    c. It was the site of the most infamous Gulag camp in Stalinist Russia.
    d. It was where the Battleship "Potemkin" was moored in 1905 when Russian sailors revolted against the Czar.
    e. It was the last battlefield of World War II where Russians invaded Japanese-occupied territory in the Far East on the last day of the war.

6 The solar calendar (365 days) came from which of the following civilizations?

    a. The Athenian Empire
    b. Court of King David
    c. Egypt's Old Kingdom
    d. The Aztec Empire
    e. The Roman Empire

7 Which one of the following colonies does not belong in this group?

    a. Botany Bay
    b. Hong Kong
    c. Norfolk Island
    d. Savannah
    e. Virginia

8 **Which of the following descriptions of Niccolo Machiavelli of Florence is inaccurate?**

a. He was tortured by the Florentine Republic late in life for his relations with the Medici family.
b. He organized and commanded a Florentine militia that fared poorly in combat in wars against the city of Pisa and Spanish forces.
c. He was a noted scholar having written *Discourses on Livy, History of Florence, Dialogue on Language* and the plays *Mandragoola* and *Clizia*.
d. His diplomatic advice inspired a brief period of unification in northern Italy in the early 16th century.
e. He served as a diplomat to the Florentine Republic.

9 **Pope Alexander VI was known for which of the following?**

a. Declaring the limits of Spanish and Portuguese territory in the New World
b. Being the subject of one of the great portraits of the Renaissance painted by Raphael
c. Asserting Spanish influence on the Papacy
d. Sleeping with his daughter Lucrezia Borgia, and sponsoring wild orgies at the Vatican
e. All of the above

10 **Which of the following events was the most devastating upheaval of the 19th century in terms of the number of lives lost?**

a. American Civil War
b. The cholera epidemic in India of 1871-72
c. The Napoleonic Wars
d. Taiping Rebellion
e. The Zulu Wars

11 **Put into correct chronological order the following Roman Emperors:**

a. Trajan
b. Antoninus Pius
c. Augustus
d. Nero
e. Tiberius

12 Which one of the following historical legends is supported by documentary evidence?

a. The use of a Trojan Horse to end the siege of Troy
b. King Arthur's Court
c. Nero fiddled while Rome burned.
d. Sir Isaac Newton's observations on gravity were based in part on the falling of an apple.
e. Robin Hood robbed from the rich and gave to the poor.

13 Rank the following British kings according to the number of illegitimate children they are believed to have fathered:

a. Charles II
b. George I
c. Henry I
d. Henry VIII
e. James II
f. John
g. William IV

14 Match the nationality with the following historical figures:

1. Catherine the Great
2. Cleopatra
3. Copernicus
4. Adolph Hitler
5. William I of England

a. Austrian
b. French
c. German
d. Greek
e. Polish

15 Match the following historical figures with their corresponding sexual attributes:

1. Augustus the Strong
2. Frederick the Great
3. Adolph Hitler
4. Lord Palmerston
5. Richard Lion-Hearted

a. Enjoyed striptease dancers and slept with his niece
b. Fathered an illegitimate child at the age of 80
c. Engaged in all-male sex orgies
d. Fathered 350 children
e. Was openly gay

16 What percentage of the German Army was transported by horses during World War II?

    a. 0 percent
    b. 10 percent
    c. 25 percent
    d. 33 percent
    e. 50 percent

17 Which of the following British monarchs was completely bald?

    a. Anne
    b. Charles I
    c. Elizabeth I
    d. George III
    e. Henry VIII

18 What Native American tribe greeted the Pilgrims at Plymouth Rock, helped them survive numerous New England winters and feasted with them in the original three-day Thanksgiving celebration?

    a. Iroquois
    b. Mohican
    c. Naragansett
    d. Pequot
    e. Wampanoag

19 Delaware was originally settled by which of the following European countries?

    a. England
    b. Denmark
    c. France
    d. Holland
    e. Sweden

20 After the United States, which was the first nation in the Americas to declare its independence from a European nation?

21 Match the following African nationalists with the nations they helped inspire toward independence from European nations:

1. Nnamdi Azikiwe   a. Ghana
2. Jomo Kenyatta   b. Kenya
3. Kwame Nkrumah   c. Nigeria
4. Julius Nyerere   d. Tanzania
5. Milton Obote   e. Uganda

22 Which of the following tribes were not part of the great Bantu expansion in pre-modern Africa?

a. Benin
b. Buganda
c. Bunyoro
d. Kikuyu
e. Lunda

23 Rank the following colonies in chronological order with reference to the dates they were permanently settled by Europeans:

a. Delaware
b. Massachusetts
c. North Carolina
d. Pennsylvania
e. Virginia

24 When the Japanese attacked the United States, several Latin American countries joined the United States in declaring war on the Axis. Which of the following nations did *not* declare war against Japan or Germany during World War II?

a. Argentina
b. Cuba
c. Haiti
d. Panama
e. Mexico

25 Match the following early 19th century Latin American nationalists with the nations or regions they are credited with leading to independence from Spain:

1. Brazil	a. Simon Bolivar
2. Chile	b. José Bonifacio de Adrada e Silva
3. Colombia & Venezuela	c. Augustin Iturbide
4. Ecuador	d. José de San Martin & Bernardo O'Higgins
5. Mexico	e. Antonio José de Sucre

26 Which South American country waged a six-year war against three of its neighboring countries in the 19th century that ended in defeat and the death of about one-half of its entire population and most of the adult male population?

a. Bolivia
b. Colombia
c. Ecuador
d. Paraguay
e. Uruguay

27 Which of the following European nations did Germany not cede territory to as a result of the Treaty of Versailles following World War I?

a. Denmark
b. France
c. Holland
d. Lithuania
e. Poland

28 When did Serbia first gain its independence in modern Europe?

a. 1815
b. 1870
c. 1878
d. 1918
e. 1991

29 What do the following men have in common: Schulyer Colfax, Henry Wilson, William Wheeler, Levi Morton and Garret Hobart?

30 Which British king said of his wife, "I had rather see toads and vipers crawling over my victuals than sit at the same table as her."?

a. Edward VII
b. Edward VIII
c. George III
d. George IV
e. Henry VIII

31 When did the Holy Roman Empire, started by Charlemagne in 800, end?

a. 1066
b. 1648
c. 1763
d. 1806
e. 1848

32 Who was the last Pope born in Rome?

a. John Paul I
b. Leo XIII
c. Paul VI
d. Pius VII
e. Pius XII

33 Who was the last ruling Albanian monarch?

a. Boris III
b. Humbert II
c. Peter II
d. Simeon II
e. Zogu I

34 What do Bob Hope, Albert Einstein, Rudolph Valentino, Irving Berlin and David Sarnoff have in common?

35 Who was Bao Dai?

   a. The Pakistani tribal commander who attacked the
      British at the Khyber Pass
   b. The first Buddhist monk to self-immolate to protest
      the Diem government in Vietnam
   c. The last monarch to rule Vietnam
   d. The King of Siam during World War II
   e. A fierce Cambodian guerrilla who led the Khmer
      Rouge for several years

36 What was the leading spectator sport in the United States in 1900?

   a. Baseball
   b. Boxing
   c. Football
   d. Horse racing
   e. Soccer

37 Where did the Philistines originate before they arrived in Palestine?

   a. Crete
   b. Syria
   c. Babylon
   d. Egypt
   e. Greece

38 Who ruled most of India in the 4th century?

   a. The Aryans
   b. The Buddhist Chin Dynasty
   c. The Hindu Gupta Empire
   d. The Huns
   e. The Persian Empire

39 Who built the Great Wall of China?

   a. Chiang Kai-shek
   b. Emperor Ch'in
   c. Emperor Wu Pi
   d. Genghis Khan
   e. Mao Tse-tung

40 Julian was considered one of the outstanding Roman emperors of the 4th century for which of the following reasons?

a. Reforming the Roman military system
b. Defeating a hard-charging barbarian army three times larger than the Roman force of 13,000 men
c. Advocating the spread of Christianity throughout Europe
d. Recapturing Britain from Celtic tribes and rebuilding the Hadrian Wall
e. Reinvigorating Rome through the advancement of education and scholarship and developing the modern calendar

41 What prevented the Mongols from conquering Continental Europe in the 13th century?

a. The Battle of Kosovo
b. The Battle of Mohacs
c. Superior weaponry and tactics of the Europeans
d. The Great Plague decimated the Mongol army.
e. Domestic politics in the Mongol Court

42 If you were in the court of Kublai in 1280, who would you likely encounter?

a. Buddha
b. Genghis Khan
c. Ivan the Terrible
d. Marco Polo
e. The Shogun

43 Which of the following countries were not created as independent states by the Treaty of Versailles in 1919?

a. Estonia
b. Finland
c. Hungary
d. Poland
e. Romania

44 Which of the following members of the Nixon administration did not go to jail as a result of the Watergate scandal?

a. Attorney General John Mitchell
b. Secretary of the Treasury Maurice Stans
c. Chief of White House Staff H. R. Bob Haldeman
d. White House Chief of Domestic Affairs John Ehrlichman
e. Counsel to the President John Dean

45 Which statement about King Philip and colonial New England is accurate?

a. A Native American chief, he waged a war that led to the complete destruction of 12 New England villages and the deaths of thousands of his people.
b. A Native American chief, he brokered a peace between warring tribes and colonialists, introducing the peace pipe to Indian-colonialist negotiations.
c. A Native American chief, he inspired his tribe to assist the Plymouth Pilgrims.
d. The King of Spain, he plundered the coast of New England, wreaking havoc on several villages.
e. The King of Spain, he started the War of Spanish Succession which resulted in fighting in New England among the British, French and Native Americans.

46 Who were the first non-Native Americans to settle in the modern-day southwestern United States?

a. Franciscan missionaries
b. Jesuit missionaries
c. Mexican soldiers
d. Spanish conquistadors
e. Russian fur traders

47 What is considered to be the first popular and uniquely American entertainment format?

a. Black minstrel shows
b. Marching bands
c. Rodeos
d. Silent movies
e. Musical comedies

48 **What was expressed in the "Seneca Falls Declaration of Sentiments" signed by 240 men and women in 1848?**

a. Men oppressed women by withholding from them the right to vote, the right to hold property and access to the educational and employment opportunities available to men, thus founding the women's suffrage movement.
b. Slavery was an abomination and a disgrace to the United States and should be abolished, thus bringing to a head the conflict between abolitionists in the North and slave holders in the South.
c. Catholic immigrants were spoiling the "American" character, thus calling on all states and the federal government to approve sweeping legislation placing restrictions on Catholics and new immigrants, starting the Know-Nothing Party.
d. The espousal of the importance of the separation of sexes and advancing the principles of the Shaker communities that were rapidly growing throughout New England and the Midwest.
e. The Mexican War was an unjust war and the United States should embrace pacifism as a national policy.

49 **What battle led to Medieval Serbia's domination, and eventual absorption, by the Ottoman Empire?**

a. The Battle of Philippopolis in 1208
b. The Battle of Velbuzd in 1330
c. The Battle of Kosovo in 1389
d. The Battle of Constantinople in 1453
e. The Battle of Agincourt in 1415

50 **When did the Islamic religion sweep through almost all of Indonesia with the exception of the Island of Bali?**

a. 13th century
b. 15th century
c. 17th century
d. 18th century
e. 19th century

51 What inspired the invention of basketball in the United States?

a. Baseball team owners' desire to create a winter sport to make even more money

b. A Springfield YMCA director's concern that attendance at his club was dropping off in the winter and his clever idea to use peach baskets and the club's existing soccer balls for an indoor winter game

c. Boredom among Union soldiers of Massachusetts during the Civil War led to the start of a game similar to modern-day basketball with seven players on a side.

d. A scholarly research paper at Amherst College in the mid-19th century that uncovered the fact that the Mayan people used to play a game with a basket and ball. The researchers decided to try the game themselves and the game subsequently became very popular.

e. Researchers do not know how the game started but believe the game first became popular in Springfield, Mass., where munitions workers played the game on vacant firing ranges.

52 Although Henry Ford started the mass production of automobiles in the United States, by the late 1920s General Motors dominated the auto industry with a 34-percent share. What unique tactic did General Motors employ?

a. Infiltrated unions with spies who broke up strikes which in other companies led to the slowdown of production. The tactic was called "union busting."

b. Started altering the models of its cars every year and completely overhauled car models every three years to prompt car owners to discard old models. The tactic was called "planned obsolescence."

c. Initiated nationwide radio and newspaper advertising campaigns to promote cars, representing the first use of electronic advertising techniques on a national scale

d. Implemented installment sales and payment plans making it easier for middle- and lower-income families to afford cars

e. Instituted the first employee-based quality improvement program

53 In 1500, where would you have found the most advanced roads and communication system?

   a. China
   b. England
   c. The Holy Roman Empire
   d. India
   e. Peru

54 Which civilization first spread the cultivation of wine throughout most of the Mediterranean?

   a. Egyptian
   b. Greek
   c. Macedonian
   d. Phoenecian
   e. Roman

55 Match the following popular substances with the source of their origin to European civilizations:

1. Cocoa	a. Native American
2. Coffee	b. Arabia
3. Opium	c. Aztecs
4. Tea	d. China
5. Tobacco	e. India

56 Timbuktu served as the commercial, learning and religious center of which of the following West African civilizations?

   a. The 11th century Ghana Empire
   b. The Berber dynasties of the 11th through 13th centuries
   c. The 14th century Mali Empire
   d. The 14th century Kanem-Bornu Empire
   e. The 15th century Benin Empire

57 Where was the first large city in North America?

   a. Mayapan
   b. Santo Domingo
   c. Santa Fe
   d. Tenochtitlan
   e. Teotihuacan

58 Who was Alfonso Albuquerque?

a. A renegade Mexican general who attempted to lead a secession effort in northern Mexico in the late 18th century
b. A Portuguese adventurer who succeeded in establishing a Portuguese trading network in the Orient in the early 1500s
c. A Spanish explorer who ventured far north of Mexico to seek the fabled "City of Gold"
d. A French duke who tried to overthrow the Mexican government
e. A Mexican traitor who assisted Texas in its war for independence

59 Match the following scientists with their corresponding historic accomplishments.

1. Nicolaus Copernicus   a. He was the first to advance the theory that the sun is the center of the universe.

2. William Harvey   b. Separately from Sir Isaac Newton, he discovered calculus.

3. Anton van Leeuwenhoek   c. He invented his own revolutionary single-lens microscope to study blood and microscopic life.

4. Gottfried Leibniz   d. He articulated the circulation of blood.

5. Andreas Vesalius   e. He broke new frontiers in medicine as the first to conduct a precise study of the human body.

60 Prior to the arrival of the British Empire in India, what was the governing power that dominated almost all of India?

a. Delhi Empire
b. Khmer Empire
c. Ming Dynasty
d. Mogul Empire
e. Mongol Empire

61 Who is considered the Father of Opera and how did he get the title?

a. Wolfgang Amadeus Mozart for his prodigious musical talents as a child and young adult who wrote the popular operas *The Marriage of Figaro, Don Giovanni* and *The Magic Flute*

b. Claudio Monteverdi for establishing opera as a secular entertainment in Italy by combining an orchestra, dramatic sets and story lines set to music

c. George Frederick Handel for composing many operatic pieces such as *Julius Caesar* that eventually became popular throughout Europe

d. Jean Baptiste Lully for combining music and song with the French court traditions of staging dances and large spectacles

e. Carlo Farinelli for his talents as a male soprano in musical pieces that popularized the operatic form. Women are said to have fainted with excitement when he sang.

62 The Factory Act of 1833 in England reformed the work laws. What were the restrictions imposed by that law?

a. Children under 9 were prohibited from working in factories and a 12-hour workday was the maximum for children aged 13-18.

b. Children under 10 were prohibited from working.

c. A 6 1/2-hour-per-day cap was placed on the work-days of children aged under 13.

d. A 12-hour-per-day cap was placed on the work days of children under 18 and all women.

e. A prohibition was placed on the use of children under age 13 in factories.

63 John Wycliff was:

a. A poet and contemporary of Geoffrey Chaucer

b. An English soldier of fortune who fought along side of the Black Prince in the Hundred Years' War

c. A religious reformer in the 14th century

d. A priest who along with Wat Tyler led the Peasants' Revolt in England in 1381

e. A wealthy English wool merchant who expanded trade with Flanders and Burgundy

64 Match the following explorers of the South Pacific with their respective accomplishments:

1. William Bligh

2. James Cook

3. Miguel Lopez de Legaspi

4. Abel Tasman

5. Samuel Wallis

a. He navigated an open boat filled with loyal British sailors who refused to mutiny on the "H.M.S. Bounty " for more than 1,000 miles.

b. A sailor for the Dutch East India Company, he discovered Tasmania off the coast of Australia.

c. He settled the Philippines as a Spanish colony.

d. He discovered Tahiti.

e. He explored much of the Australian coast, visited the Antarctic and discovered numerous islands in the South Pacific including Hawaii.

65 Well connected. Which one of the following contemporaries was not known to have met any of the other four?

a. Henry VIII, King of England
b. Leonardo da Vinci, Italian artist
c. Martin Luther, German religious reformer
d. Albrecht Dürer, German painter and engraver
e. Francis I, King of France

66 Which statement about the Marquis de Lafayette is not true?

a. He was a general in the American Continental Army in 1777.
b. He was a member of the French National Assembly and Commander of the National Guard at the beginning of the French Revolution in 1789.
c. He was declared a traitor and fled France in 1792.
d. He became Marshall of the Grand Army of the Republic under Napoleon in 1802.
e. He commanded the National Guard during the Revolution of 1830.

Genius Answers

(Score 1 point for each correct answer unless otherwise indicated.)

1.   Virgin Islands cost $7.5 million, Alaska $7.2 million. (1/2 point for which was more expensive; 1/2 point for price differential.)

2. c   MacArthur rarely, if ever, carried a sidearm in Korea even when entering combat areas.

3. d

4. a   Alexander first distinguished himself as a youngster by taming Bucephelus after much older and more experienced horse trainers failed.

5. c   The Kolyma Basin is located in Far Eastern Russia and was the most infamous site of the Gulag in Stalinist Russia. Of the 12 to 15 million people killed in labor camps, Kolyma accounted for about one-fifth. Working in minus 50-degree Fahrenheit temperatures at times, prisoners were forced to mine for gold.

6. c

7. b   All the others were destination sites for British prisoners.

8. d   Italy was never united during Machiavelli's lifetime and the advice put forth in *The Prince* in 1513 was largely ignored by his contemporaries.

9. e

10. d   The Taiping Rebellion of 1850 resulted in the deaths of an estimated 20 million people, roughly equal to the entire population of Great Britain at the time. The Chinese population revolted against the Ch'ing Dynasty of foreign Manchurians who had ruled the nation for two centuries. At the conclusion of the rebellion 14 years later, the dynasty was severely weakened, making China vulnerable to European influences.

11. c   Augustus (27 B.C. - 14 A.D.); e. Tiberius (14 A.D. - 37); d. Nero (54-68); a. Trajan (98-117); b. Antoninus Pius (138-161)

12. d

13. c,   a, g, f, e, b, d   Henry I (21); Charles II (14); William IV (11); John (8); James II (6); George I (4); Henry VIII (1) (3 points)

14. 1c,   2d,   3e,   4a,   5b (1/2 point each)

15. 1d,   2c,   3a,   4b,   5e (1/2 point each)

16. e

17. c Elizabeth I suffered from a disease early in her life that led to the loss of her hair.

18. e
19. e
20. Haiti. Under the leadership of the former slave Toussaint L'Overture, Haiti declared its independence from France in 1801. Haiti gained its independence in 1804 but meanwhile L'Overture had been captured and thrown in a French dungeon where he died in 1803.

21. 1c, 2b, 3a, 4d, 5e (1/2 point each)
22. a
23. e, b, a, c, d Virginia (1606), Massachusetts (1620), Delaware (1638), North Carolina (1653), Pennsylvania (1682)

24. a
25. 1b, 2d, 3a, 4e, 5c (1/2 point each)
26. d
27. c
28. c
29. They all served as United States vice-presidents in the late 19th century.

30. d
31. d The Holy Roman Empire came to an end in 1806 when Napoleon, through the Confederation of the Rhine, bound to him the remaining German states that made up the Empire.

32. e
33. e
34. They all passed through Ellis Island as immigrants to the United States.

35. c
36. b
37. a
38. c
39. b An emperor of the Ch'in dynasty, the first to unify China built the Great Wall in the 2nd Century BC as a defense against marauding warriors from the north.

40. b
41. e After having swept European armies aside from the Baltic Sea to the Danube River in a month-long campaign, the Mongol armies suddenly withdrew because the Mongol princes had to return home to select a new leader after the ruling Khan, Ogdai, died.

42. d
43. e
44. a
45. c
46. b
47. a
48. a
49. c
50. b
51. b
52. b
53. e
54. b
55. 1c, 2b, 3e, 4d, 5a
56. c
57. e   Located in central Mexico, this city flourished from about 100 BC to 600 AD, reaching a population as high as 200,000. Remnants of the city can be seen today where massive pyramids and a giant plaza still stand.
58. b
59. 1a, 2d, 3c, 4b, 5e (1/2 point each)
60. d
61. b
62. a
63. c   John Wycliff was a master at Oxford whose religious beliefs contributed to the Peasants' Revolt (let by Wat Tyler and John Ball) but he did not partcipate in the revolt.
64. 1a, 2e, 3c, 4b, 5d (1/2 point each)
65. c
66. d